Chu Jeng's Willow Palm
Copyright © Kevin B. Shearer
Illustrated by Kevin B. Shearer II

ISBN-13: 978-1974227129

ISBN-10: 197422712X

i

**To everyone who seeks
the higher path
of the righteous warrior**

WILLOW PALM

The First Defensive Set
of Chu Jeng's Basic Form, Zephyr

The Power of Willow Palm

Willow Palm is a unique and uniquely powerful blocking set of Wind Fist Kung Fu. Creative freedom and greatly enhanced defense were some of the first effects I noticed in those who had learned Willow Palm, but there was more to come; far more! The daily practice of Willow Palm gave my students a fluidity of motion that had five wonderful effects on them:

THE FIRST of these resultant effects was **increased efficiency**. The free fluidity of Willow Palm helps martial artists to relax. Relaxation, especially in the antagonistic muscles of any motion, allows the practitioner to expend less energy; thus tiring less rapidly. A very accomplished martial artist, just like an accomplished gymnast, or boxer, or tennis player, or any other athlete, makes his work look effortless. That effortless appearance is always the result of the efficiency that comes with relaxation, especially of antagonistic tension. When you are throwing a straight punch, the deltoids, triceps

1

and pectorals are primarily responsible for driving the punch forward, and any tension in the biceps and latisimus dorsi will restrict the punch, slowing it down and wasting your energy.

> He who tires in battle will die in that same battle.

A greater warrior who is exhausted can be defeated by a far lesser fighter who is fresh. As they say; "He who tires in battle will die in that same battle." The best generals of ancient times knew this and developed ways of switching out troops to keep their best from being defeated by lesser men. But in a street fight, you will not have a great general to switch you out when you grow tired. That's where smooth, relaxed efficiency comes in for you.

The movements of Willow Palm are, with the exception of very few instantaneous points, very relaxed and efficient. This emphasis on relaxation in the set gives rise to the same non-antagonistic relaxation in all the rest of a martial artist's techniques, if he practices Willow Palm properly and diligently. And that enhanced relaxation always leads to more efficient use of the muscles and a critically important preservation of energy in a fight.

THE SECOND resultant effect of the daily practice of Willow Palm is **increased power**. Any advanced martial artist understands the effects of sudden tension in a strike, or even in a hard block. This sudden tension is most often said to occur at the "point of impact," but we Dragons say it comes at the "point of penetration" into the target. Just words, one might say, but words have a huge defining effect on one's mind and a huge expressive effect in one's actions. A spitwad may impact, but an arrow penetrates. See the difference? And a punch cannot suddenly tense into a target if it is already tense. I won't offer an artificial numerical percentage, but it is true that a huge percentage of a martial artist's strikes deliver power through the sudden tension into the target beginning at the point of penetration.

There is no sense in exploding a missile before it reaches the target and no sense in tensing into a punch before it reaches the target. It may go without saying that something that is already tense cannot be tensed, but this critical point must be emphasized, because it is a difficult thing for most people to achieve. Willow Palm, *can* help you to achieve this powerful effect, and

> There is no sense in exploding the missile before it reaches the target.

I have seen the wonderful empowering results of it over and over throughout the years. Though Willow Palm is a defensive—or blocking—set, it lends profound relaxation to all of a martial artist's movements, thereby increasing his opportunity to tense his hits into a target with a massively increased delivery of real power.

THE THIRD resultant effect of the daily practice of Willow Palm is **increased confidence**. Confidence, courage, hope and faith are all virtues of a related nature, and critically important to any fighter. Hope gives life to effort, and we have all seen the doomed efforts of those who struggle on without these virtues. It is true, that the practice of

> Hope gives life to effort.

martial arts can build these virtues in a diligent practitioner, but it is common in martial artists to have doubts, from time to time, about the completeness of their art. I have consistently seen Willow Palm give my students a unique sort of creative freedom in their defenses that nothing else does. This creative freedom quickly gives rise to a good, measured confidence that has them swatting away attacks in effective ways that are often unique to their own character, often surprising even themselves.

THE FOURTH resultant effect of the daily practice of Willow Palm is an amazing increase of the martial artist's **adaptability**. No fighting system could possibly encompass in its curriculum all possibilities that may arise in the realm of personal combat. It's just impossible. It has been wrongly attributed to Charles Darwin that, "It is not the strongest species that survives, but the most adaptable." Regardless of who originated that truth, it is true. We have to be adaptable in a fight, unless we are all knowing, and none of us are. Along with other good practices, Willow Palm gives this freeing power of adaptability more than anything else I have ever seen.

> It is not the strongest that survive, but the most adaptable.

Adaptability enables a fighter to avoid playing the enemy's favorite game. For instance; if he likes long range, you go short, and vise versa. If he is complex, you go simple, and vise versa. If he is strong, you avoid a contest of strength. Without the virtue of adaptability, you are stuck in frozen, limited patterns that may not be the best thing for the situation in which you find yourself. But Willow Palm is a pattern that naturally causes a practitioner to reach out beyond the pattern itself and adapt to the situation at hand.

THE FIFTH resultant effect of the daily practice of Willow Palm is a marked increase of **unpredictability**. There are many excellent martial art styles out there, but most of them are predictable to some degree, many of them very much so. That predictability is a weakness. Those who practice Wind Fist are known for their unpredictability. Each of them is very different from the others, and on any given day each of them may fight very differently from the way he fought the day before. I believe this unpredictability comes chiefly from Willow Palm, as I have seen it give this quality to advanced black belts of other styles very soon after I taught it to them. It is difficult for an opponent to start off by denying you your game when he cannot predict what game you are going to play. And it is even better when your game changes before he has even caught on to the first phase of it.

As far as the observable effects of Willow Palm, I will offer you two anecdotal incidents to consider, as they are just two of the countless examples of Willow Palm's power. One day, a teenage brown belt who studied at another good school, where his father was a black belt instructor came for a group

> "Wishing the world was predictable and controllable does not make it so, and it might make us disregard what is actually happening."
>
> -Jean G. Boulton

lesson at our school. In that one lesson, I taught the young man Willow Palm. He returned to his own school the next night and mopped the floor with every black belt in the place. His father was furious and told him, "You can't ever go to that school again!" Imagine that. If my son went to another school for one lesson and came back to handily defeat all of us, I would beg to go to that school myself and learn whatever he had learned. But then, every martial artist studies for different reasons; not all of them for function.

The second incident involves a young deputy sheriff to whom I had taught Willow Palm. He got involved in a car chase with a criminal, who then abruptly stopped his car and ran back to fight with the lone officer. The fight raged on as a lady looked out her door and called 911. I was on duty that night and raced to his aid along with many other officers. When we arrived, the bad guy was already in cuffs and the officer unharmed. I asked the deputy what happened during the long fight. He said the guy came running back at him, raging and swinging like a boxer. I asked him if he had gotten hit. He gave me a quizzical look, patted his body as if in thought, then exclaimed, "No! I guess he never even touched me in all that! But my forearms and wrists are really sore."

I laughed with joy, because it was obvious that Willow Palm had done its magic and intercepted every blow, probably saving that officer's life. His wrists were sore from sweeping enemy blows aside, rather than his body being sore from receiving them, or him being dead from getting beaten down, disarmed and killed with his own sidearm, as happens all too often to our officers.

What Willow Palm is Designed to Protect

Fights are most often wild, frenzied events, so you can forget about trying to locate some "vital striking point" three inches below and two-point-five inches to the left of the attacker's left nipple. It may sound laughable, but I have seen such charts of "vital striking points" available for sale in the back of martial art magazines, and for top dollar. Save your money and punch for the enemy's center. But it gets just a bit more technical than that, and is still very workable in a fight, without having to get out a ruler and ask your attacker to stand still.

The human body has natural hard points and more vulnerable points, according to good, solid rules of common sense. For instance, those areas that are less apt to be subject to impact are more sensitive to impact, such as the armpits. Those areas that are more commonly impacted in the daily course of life, such as the palms of the hands, the bottoms of the feet and the kneecaps, are more suited to endure impact. The parts of the body that are the most vital to life are generally protected, but still vulnerable to good solid hits, such as the heart, diaphragm, brain, carotid artery and others.

Now, keep in mind that we do not hit to annoy or punish our attackers. We hit to stop. It's the same for police officers. They are not authorized to shoot somebody in the knee or the hand. They only have the right to shoot into vital areas in order to stop the perpetrator from doing something worse than them shooting him, such as killing an innocent victim. They shoot to stop, not to wing, or wound or persuade. That is why *every* shot an officer takes is considered the use of "deadly force." Shooting to stop is basically shooting to kill.

We hit to stop. We don't hit to prove something or to entertain ourselves, but to stop an attacker from attacking us. And the best way to stop a determined attacker is to immediately disrupt one of his major bodily functions. We do that by blasting too much force into an area called The Deadly Band in too little space and too little time for him to absorb without his function as an attacker to be disrupted. That doesn't mean punching him in a hardened area that has nothing to do with his life functions, such as the hip or shoulder. It means punching him in the heart, solar plexus, liver, spleen, spine, brain, eyes, throat, neck, etcetera. And all of these reasonable, effective targets can be found right there on The Deadly Band. The only other main target area we use is called The Cross, which is the line that crosses The Deadly Band all the way around the body across the diaphragm, kidneys and spine. It is very easy to target these vital areas in a fight, and it is not hard to protect them with the fast sweeping parries of Willow Palm.

The illustration below shows the deadly band target area (in gray) as well as the starting position for Willow Palm.

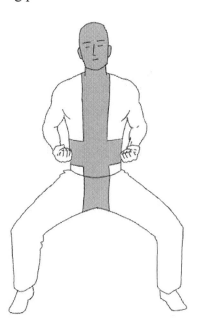

PREPARATION

We practice this defensive set, Willow Palm, from the Square Horse Stance, which is only used for practice. The feet are flat on the floor and parallel to each other with the knees directly over the toes as if you were riding on a horse. Fists are at your ribs and your back is straight up. It is very important that you press your knees outward and keep your lower legs looking straight up from the front, but they will actually lean forward the exact length of your foot from heel to knee.

As noted, the Square Horse Stance is a practice stance. You will learn the Fighting Horse Stance, and many other fighting stances, in the third set of Zephyr, called Bedrock.

The Square Horse Stance

The Structure of Willow Palm

So then, keeping in mind that you are to practice Willow Palm in a relaxed manner, let us begin. The first movement of the set is called the **Reverse Parry** as illustrated in the sequence below from left to right:

The starting position and finish position for the Reverse Parry are shown here:

It is very important that you extend your arm all the way forward in this midpoint of the Reverse Parry. This is where you want to first contact your enemy's wrist with the back of your hand and pull it off past your shoulder, not when his punch is an inch from your face.

You begin in the Square Horse practice stance with your fists at your hips (palm upward). As in the illustrations above, you open one fist and bring it to the opposite side in a sweeping arc from low to high slinging the incoming punch to the side by pulling back to your shoulder. Do not be tempted to push your hand outward to the side.

It will not work that way because you do not have the leverage to do so. You do, however, have the power to pull to your shoulder from the opposite corner (a point as far as you can reach, without twisting your torso, directly in front of the opposite shoulder). This movement should catch the enemy's punch by the wrist with the back of your left hand and sling it far to the side without you having to push it outward. It is very important to catch the incoming weapon with the back of your hand or wrist and sling it outward by pulling back across your deadly band. Don't wait until the punch is close, and make sure you time your Reverse Parry to the speed of the enemy's punch. Be sure to catch the enemy's weapon out near arm's length before it gets too close to you. The object is to catch the incoming punch by the wrist, not the hand, and sling it away. If you are catching his wrist six inches from your nose, then your nose has already gotten punched.

The second movement of the set is called the **Parry Thrust**. This block is more linear and forceful than the Reverse Parry, but is not stiff or rigid, especially after its completion.

From the end of the reverse Parry you thrust your hand straight across from that shoulder to as far as you can reach directly in front of your opposite shoulder, pushing the enemy's weapon to the side with the palm of your hand. Do this without twisting your shoulders or folding your hand or separating your fingers. Keep your hand vertical and in the form of the last leaf on a flexible willow branch. Like the Reverse Parry, your Parry Thrust will cross your deadly band and stop just at the outside edge of your opposite shoulder as illustrated in the sequence below:

At the end of this parry, your hand is thrust as far out in front of your opposite shoulder as can be without turning your body. Always do this parry with your thumb and fingers together and straight, but as you catch an attacker's wrist with the palm of your hand, your hand will naturally conform to his wrist and give you greater control, but do not try to do this artificially, or you will put your fingers at risk of injury. Just thrust him away from you with your flattened palm and let nature take its course in the shape of your hand at the moment it clashes with the enemy's wrist.

The starting position and finish position for the Parry Thrust are shown here:

The Parry Thrust is not a sweeping circular movement like the Reverse Parry, but a linear thrusting movement, and involves a bit more physical force and tension. But be sure to relax your hand and arm as soon as you finish thrusting the weapon off target.

The third movement of the set is called the **Parry**, which is shown in two illustrations here, though it is one smooth sweeping movement from far out in front of your opposite shoulder to rest at your opposite shoulder.

The Parry sweeps in to your opposite shoulder (from in front of the shoulder of the hand used) to slap the enemy's wrist away with the palm of your hand as shown in the following sequence:

You must always sweep the incoming weapon off your deadly band for these parries to be effective.

The farthest point of the effective Parry sweep is out in front of the same shoulder as the hand used, as indicated by the star in the photo below:

The starting position and finish position for the Parry are shown here:

There is really no tension in this block. It sweeps through the enemy's wrist and throws his weapon to the side in a relaxed manner as your hand returns to your shoulder. Meet the incoming blow far out with your palm and guide it off as you return.

The fourth movement of the set is called the **Outward Parry**. Rather than your palm or the back of your hand, you will use the blade (side) of your hand to sweep the enemy's weapon arm aside. This is a very long block and can stop the enemy's punch by stopping any part of his arm, even at his shoulder if you are very fast, but the optimal form is to catch his wrist as in the other parries of this set. As you can see in the short sequence below, this is a very simple, but effective, parry:

As the sequence is so short, a start and finish photo is not necessary for this parry. Like the Parry Thrust, the Outward Parry ends all the way out in front of one of your shoulders, and is more forceful than the relaxed sweeping type of parries. But do not tense up too much or remain tensed after the Outward Parry has done its work. This is critically important. You

You must relax. There is about as much tension in Kung Fu as there is punctuation in a sentence.

must relax. There is about as much tension in Kung Fu as there is punctuation in a sentence.

As a side note, I will say that the relaxation you gain from Kung Fu practice will do more for your health and happiness than most anything else you might ever do.

The fifth movement of the set is called the **Crane Parry**. The handform is an imitation of the White Crane's neck, head and beak. Press the tip of your thumb to the tip of your middle finger and press all other fingertips against those to keep them all safe (they are much stronger together than any of them could be alone). The Crane Parry is a sweeping parry that catches the enemy's wrist and gives you good control of his arm, enabling you to easily sweep it to the side. Though shown low to the outside in Willow Palm, the Crane Parry can be done high or low and to the outside or to the inside. Low Crane Parries can also allow you catch an enemy's kick and toss him off balance. You should do Willow Palm in front of a mirror from time to time in order to check and perfect your positions. Note that you can see just a little air between the elbow and the body when the Crane Parry is completed in the sequence below:

The Crane Parry shown here is used to sweep a low blow to the side and off your deadly band. The critical point, as in all blocks, is to keep any blow from striking into your deadly band or cross area, but you want to keep all weapons off any part of your body other than the part with which you are blocking, such as your palm or wrist. Defense is always more important than attack. You must not let the enemy strike you!

The Crane Parry start and finish positions are shown here:

Note that the hand must sweep high across the body from the position of the last parry in order to sweep across the lower deadly band to this final position.

(Were it the opposite Low Crane Parry, which you should be able to figure out, it would drop on its own side and sweep across the lower deadly band to the opposite side. But it is not advised that you experiment with it until you know the whole set very well.)

At the end of this book, you will be shown the entire sequence of Willow Palm from start to finish, and again from the side so that you can more easily understand the long range of these blocks.

The sixth movement of the set is called the **Dragon Tail Parry**. In this parry, you sweep across your deadly band to toss an enemy's punch out by the wrist with the inside bone of your own wrist. At the end of the movement, your wrist is aligned with the outside of your shoulder and your hand is palm up and pointed forward as if you were balancing a board on your shoulder and hand, as shown in the following sequence:

This parry is a much closer range parry than most of the parries in Willow Palm, as you will see in the final sequence of this book. It is a lot like the classic Outward Block, which is done in most styles and you will learn in the Oak Wrist book after this one. It is like that block, but faster and more relaxed, though it is a bit more tensed than most of the other parries. The open

> The open hand of the Dragon Tail Parry helps you to stay relaxed.

hand of the Dragon Tail Parry helps you to stay more relaxed than if it were clenched in a fist as in the Outward Block, and relaxation, as already noted, is most important.

Note in the illustration below, that the final position of the Dragon Tail Parry has your forearm aligned with the outside of your body and the fingers pointed straight forward with the palm up. This is to ensure that you clash the inner bone of your wrist against your enemy's arm rather than your more vulnerable muscles and tendons against his bone. The clash of bone and softer tissue is not a necessary concern in the softer sweeping parries. This is a very important consideration which you should think about and apply throughout your training.

The seventh movement of the set is called the **Downward Parry**. This parry is used to thrust a kick or very low punch downward with the palm of your hand. For the safety of your wrist you MUST keep a slight bend in your elbow when blocking a kick in order to provide a bit of shock reduction. DO NOT attempt to block a mid body punch or kick downward or upward. Any strike that comes in between your belt and collar bone must be blocked to the side, unless you accompany that block with a backward movement.

It is hard to see in the sequence shown above, but the final position of the Downward Parry is rather far out from your groin area. This is because it is used most often to block a kick at the ankle, and the length of the foot would have the enemy's toes still crashing into your groin if you blocked too close to your body.

The eighth movement of the set is called the **Upward Parry**. This parry is only used against a punch to your head or neck, and never against a punch below your collar bones, as that might direct the enemy's fist into your face. You push the punch up by the wrist (with the palm of your hand) while it is far out in front of you, as shown in the sequence below:

All that is needed is to clear the enemy's punch from hitting your head, as shown above, but there are times that we thrust the enemy's arm very high overhead.

The Upward Parry can be a more circular sweeping parry or a more linear thrusting block, and we do use it both ways as needed. In this particular sequence, the parry is harder, more linear and tense than when it is done as a long sweeping parry. But remember, as always, to relax once you have finished the movement.

Note that your fingers are pointed straight to the side of the arm you are using. This is the best configuration for using the power of your muscles in such an upward movement. It helps to keep your fingers from being jammed and gives a larger surface with which to intercept the enemy's wrist.

The ninth movement of the set is called **Pass Through the Guard**. The guard position is formed by placing the last section of your index finger in the dip between the deltoid muscle and the pectoral muscle of your opposite shoulder. But you do not stop there in the Willow Palm set. Just pass through the guard on your way to putting both fists at your ribs, as shown in the sequence below:

In the guard position, which is used when we are in the Fighting Horse Stance, has the forearm protecting the cross area of the deadly band. The arm is about a fist away from the body, so that a heavy blow, such as a kick, would not transfer its force through our own arm into the vulnerable cross area.

You should practice Willow Palm every day, without fail. It is a very short and easy set, but will give your defenses an amazing boost if you are faithful and diligent. Do it every day at least once per day, preferably many times a day. Keep in mind that it is our habits that form us into what we are, not the occasional things we do.

Stay very relaxed as you practice and always imagine the enemy's punches coming in and your hands sweeping or thrusting them off of you, at least off of your deadly band. Do this faithfully and you will gain very much from it. Remember that, like everything you do in life, you get out of it what you put into it.

And don't block out too far to the side. Generally keep your elbows close enough to protect your ribs. There is no need to block way out to the side as if you need the enemy's punch to miss you be five feet. Beginners often think this kind of immoderate excessively wide blocking keeps them safer, but it does just the opposite and leaves them vulnerable and in danger. Notice in the sequence below how the blocks only toss the enemy weapons off the body enough to clear them off of you. The hands should never extend way out beyond the sides of the body. It's a matter of courage and self-discipline that pays off very well in the end, if you can manage it, and YOU CAN if you really want to.

The idea is to practice Willow Palm until the powers, particulars and principles of this uniquely powerful defensive set become instinctive for you. Then, when an unavoidable fight occurs, you should be able to block instantly and without thinking.

Experienced Kung Fu practitioners understand that human beings have no instincts for fighting. They know that the ancient masters imitated animal fighting movements and adapted them to the human body to create the original Kung Fu fighting styles. And by imitating good, solid fighting movements developed by those who are both experienced and knowledgeable, we gain, over time, something very much like animal instincts. It doesn't mean you are going to rip somebody's head off for trying to brush lint off your shoulder, but that you will have what it takes when you really come to need it. It's all about gaining good fighting instincts and acting according to the justice known by our well-ordered human spirits.

Opposite is the entire Willow Palm sequence from the front:

Here is the entire Willow Palm sequence from the side so that you may see the long distances of the sweeping parries:

The Philosophy of Willow Palm

Ultimately, Willow Palm is about freedom and adaptability, and that is precisely what it will give you if you work hard at it. Once you have done it thousands of times, while trying to make every repetition of the set better than the last time you did it, you will find many great powers hidden within. Some of these will become apparent to you as time goes on and you learn more of Chu Jeng's other powerful basic sets and some of the other fighting forms we will present to you in future books. But one of these hidden powers I will reveal to you now:

Consider the sequence of the Reverse Parry followed by the Parry Thrust. It seems to be pure defense, but it is so much more than that. Imagine a man stepping toward you and throwing a left punch at your head. You should step back with your left foot as you bring your left hand to guard at your right shoulder as you sweep his weapon off to your right side with the back of your right hand or wrist by pulling your right Reverse Parry from far out in front of your left shoulder in close to your right shoulder. Now, in the Willow Palm set, the next move would be to shoot your right hand out in a Parry Thrust. But instead of that, shoot your right hand out in the same motion, punching him in the head or chopping him in the neck.

It's an ancient high principle of Kung Fu that any attack can be a defense just as any defense can be an attack.

It can be the same going from Parry to Outward Parry or most any other part of the sequence. Investigate this thoroughly and you will find many treasures of freedom and power hidden within. If you are already an accomplished martial artist, this investigation will be easier and more productive for you. But we will have more books forthcoming to help you with that and to teach you the stances, hand strikes, kicks, hard blocks and advanced fighting patterns to make this martial path all the more clear and productive for you.

The History of Willow Palm

The exact dates are unknown, but I believe I was sixteen when Willow Palm came to me. That would make it about 1975. I left Golden Gloves boxing and began studying martial arts in 1971 under Frank Gutierrez in Tucson, Arizona. He held black belts in Judo, Tae Kwon Do and Shoto Kan Karate, as well as a blue belt in Aikido. Sensei Gutierrez combined these arts into his own style, which he called Wun Hop Ryu Kan. I studied under him for a year and a half, but Willow Palm did not arise directly from what I studied with that good man, though without his influence it never would have come about.

Toward the end of my study with him, Sensei Gutierrez took his school to an open tournament. It was a very large tournament and many schools competed in it. Those were the days when the fights were bare-fisted and very rough. Throughout that day I watched with extreme disappointment as the Kenpo students from other schools took every single fighting trophy in every division. I asked my Sensei how that could happen. He replied, "It's just because there are so many of them." I will never forget those words, or the thoughts and feelings they induced in me, for as long as I live.

I was only thirteen at the time, but the flaw in that statement was painfully apparent to me: the number of contestants is irrelevant, because we each fight when rested and only face one at a time. One fact pressed in on my mind and I could not deny it: *The Kenpo guys were better than we were!* That's all there was to it, and I had clearly seen it during their performances in the ring.

I loved Sensei Gutierrez and am eternally grateful to him for giving me a good start in the martial arts, but there was only one thing for me to do. A week later, I was studying Kenpo at a school that would later be called, the Chinese Martial Arts Association. After studying the relatively stiffer Japanese arts, I was thrilled at the fluidity and diversity of movement inherent in Kenpo, which is an Americanized Chinese Art. The school eventually hired me to teach, and I began that lifelong endeavor on the day after my eighteenth birthday.

During those early years, I fervently practiced for four hours every day. I worked at Kenpo most of all, but studied other arts with many different teachers and practitioners on the sly, sacrificing nearly every other aspect of my life for advancement in the martial arts. One evening, it came to me to put the soft parries of Kenpo, and a few from the other styles I was studying, together into a little blocking set. It looked a bit like the last leaf on the long supple branches of a weeping willow tree blowing in the wind. Thus the name; Willow Palm. At the time, it felt good to do it, but I had no idea of the wonderful power and freedom that would later come of it.

A few years later I had many good students at the Chinese Martial Arts Association studying directly under me. When sparring with them I could set my weapons on them whenever I wanted, but they could rarely get though my defenses at all. The thought never occurred to me that my secret Willow Palm set was the reason. Eventually I decided to teach one of my students the set. The very next time I sparred with her, her hands were everywhere and swatting my weapons away with great freedom and finesse. Her blocks were suddenly like a thick swarm of bees! It was very difficult to get through at all, and there was nothing other than Willow Palm to explain the sudden dramatic change.

Those who ran the school routinely ridiculed all other styles and dismissed as worthless anything from any martial art other than Kenpo; so I never brought up Willow Palm or even mentioned it to them. I secretly taught a few of my favorite students the set and got them to agree to keep it a secret. The owners of the school never figured out how or why those particular students suddenly acquired such formidable and adaptive defenses. With each of them, it was like an overnight miracle, and the confused, amazed and frustrated expressions on the higher ranking faces at the school made me very happy with what I had secretly developed and given to my students.

Over the years I refined, adapted and expanded Willow Palm into several manifestations, and found each one of them to be exceedingly beneficial. One of them is tremendously powerful, but is over fifty movements long! Few people want to ever delve that deep into the study, even if they do understand that **Kung Fu means hard work.**

Style or System?

(an essay on the essence of study in the martial arts)

People talk about some particular martial art "style" being better or lesser than another, but they don't know what they're talking about.

Any "stye" is only a part of a system of becoming that is particular to a school, teacher, practice methods, philosophy, student body, individual student, culture, and many other elements that contribute to, or detract from, the personal changes accomplishable by a student.

The "system" would be better understood as a "situation" that enables the change. The study of a martial art or, as is far more often the case, a combative sport, is not exactly like the study of math, or language, or hard science, though it is not completely different. The successful study of a martial art is a matter of BECOMING, rather than just filling one's head with a particular kind of knowledge.

Optimally, the style itself is comprised largely of a set of techniques and/or forms, which are based in the physical sciences. That is to say they are designed to use the human body as powerfully and efficiently as possible according to the laws of physics, in order to control the exchange of energy in a personal physical confrontation.

So a "good style" is all about providing a SITUATION that will best enable the student to become fast, powerful, well-balanced, maneuverable, perceptive, deceptive and adaptable in a fight. These qualities could be further broken down, but that is not the purpose of this essay.

Now, obviously, some styles are better suited to certain body types, personalities, mentalities and lifestyles than are others. But, as noted above, there is more to the "situation of becoming" than just the style, or body of physical knowledge. Practice methods, school culture, system philosophy, moral discipline, training tools and school spirit have a huge impact on what the student is likely to become in the process of his study.

Points to consider in the greater "situation" of a particular martial art study:

• If the situation is limited in scope, then the student is most likely to become limited in his approach to fighting.

• If the situation is nebulous and ill-defined, then the student is likely to become confused and uncertain in his approach to fighting.

• If the situation is dogmatic and rigid, then the student is most likely to become dogmatic, rigid, unadaptable and unthinking in his approach to fighting.

• If the system is immoral, violent or prideful, then the student is most likely to become immoral, selfish, cowardly and bullying in his approach to fighting.

• If the system is soft and weak, then the student is most likely to become soft, weak and incapable in his approach to fighting.

• If the system is malfunctional, that is; containing techniques, basics and elements that just do not work, then the student is most likely to become deluded in his approach to fighting and be very unpleasantly surprised when he gets into his first serious fight.

• If the system is underdeveloped or totally lacking (as nearly all styles are) in philosophy and strategy, then the student is most likely to remain immature and ignorant in his approach to fighting.

• If the system is narrowly suited to a particular mind set or body type, then the student is most likely to never become capable in his approach to fighting unless he happens to personally match that particular mind set or body type, which, given the vast variance in human beings, is quite unlikely.

> If the system is narrowly suited to a particular mindset or body type, then the student is most likely to never become capable in his approach to fighting unless he happens to personally match that particular mindset and body type.

• If the system is diverse in its curriculum, as is Wind Fist Kung Fu, then the student is most likely to find his own niche according to his particular mind set and body type and become powerful in his approach to fighting.

• If the system is diverse and widely varied in its training and practice methods, as is Wind Fist Kung Fu, then the student is most likely to become adaptable and unpredictable in his approach to fighting, and less likely to be surprised or predicted by an opponent or stumped by something "new" in a fight.

• If the system is well-rooted in a deep, rational, comprehensive philosophy, as is Wind Fist Kung Fu, then the student is most likely to become wise, intelligent and quite formidable in his approach to fighting.

• If the system is moral and responsible in its practices and expectations, as is Wing Fist Kung Fu, then the student is most likely to become a moral and responsible person in his approach to fighting.

Now, please consider that what a serious student becomes in regard to fighting, he will most certainly become in his approach to life itself and his relationships with all other human beings. Any intelligent and observant person who has studied a martial art in a significant way will know this to be true.

Now, you might ask, "Are there really systems that are nebulous and ill-defined, dogmatic and rigid, immoral, violent or prideful, soft and weak, malfunctional, underdeveloped or totally lacking in philosophy or narrowly suited to a particular mind set or body type?" The answer is yes. Unfortunately many martial art systems out there suffer from at least one of these defects, and do not know it. In fact, the knee-jerk justification of a "superior-to-all-others" style, usually comes from an insecurity, which causes them to subjugate their reason to their desire, thereby assuring that they will never discover the truth and correct their mistakes. Now, are all martial artists like this? No, they are not, but it is often difficult to find one that is not.

And, "Why" you might ask, "is Wind Fist Kung Fu free from these defects?" That is a legitimate and very important question to ask, because I could be just another insecure martial artist trying to convince you that his art is better than all the others. First off, I don't really know that Wind Fist Kung Fu is better than all the others, because I have not studied or even seen ALL the others. Nobody on earth has. But I have studied seventeen different styles under twenty-eight teachers over the years, and watched, observed, competed against or read about many other styles in practice and talked to their teachers and practitioners.

Furthermore, my abhorrence of blind justification, dishonesty and subjecting reason to desire started very early in life and guided my way in creating Wind Fist Kung Fu.

Some time after earning my black belt in Kenpo, I tore the system apart and combined it with many of the other styles I had studied. I was totally ruthless in subjugating every element to functionality above all else. I kept what worked well and tossed out, or modified, what did not work, to the point that only about forty-five percent of our system still bears a resemblance to Kenpo. But no Kenpo artist would ever look at our system and say, "That's Kenpo." That new system, I called Wind Fist Kung Fu, because it is as adaptable as the wind and it conforms to the nature and practices of the styles of Kung Fu I studied more than anything else. Inseparable from the physical curriculum of Wind Fist Kung Fu is the teaching

"A teacher that could make you an invincible fighter, but teach you nothing about character and inner strength is a teacher from which to flee as from a burning building."

— Akiyama Munenoshi

Brotherhood that it is built into: Lung Tong. After studying the histories of some of the Chinese Tongs and the Knights Hospitaller and other benevolent organizations, I formed this society to promote, guard and preserve the teachings, materials, practice methods, strategies, moral principles and philosophies I developed and adapted to our system. Wind Fist Kung Fu and Lung Tong are essential and inseparable major parts of the whole system of becoming that, as far as any one of us has seen, has no equal in this world, but then, we haven't seen everything.

I accomplished all of this by ruthlessly subjecting my personal desires to well-informed reason for the objective of discovering the truth and the functional principles of personal combat. And I created a unique and diverse martial art system of "becoming" that has proven itself time and time again to be amazingly effective in enabling people of a very wide range of personalities and body types to become exceptionally capable fighters in a short time and then, after lengthy study, reach heights of ability almost never seen in any martial artist of any style.

King Solomon asked God for wisdom instead of riches, and so God gave him both wisdom and riches without measure. In a smaller but similar way, I did not seek to make the "toughest" fighting art, but wanted more than anything else to create a system that would enable people of good will to develop their full natures in a powerful and healthy way through a martial path. And, because of my choice, I was given a true martial art of amazing power along with the fine system of personal development that I sought. All experiences we have had on the street, up against other martial artists and in the conflicts of life have fully born this truth out. I'm not saying I have any reason to be proud of what I have done, and I am not. I was only the lucky conduit through which it happened. All I can say is that I stood on the shoulders of giants who came before me and saw the truth from that great vantage point.

In conclusion: When a martial artist claims his style is "the best there is" there is a very great chance that he is just expressing a desperate desire without a single thought to reason or a love of the truth. He most likely has no concept of the whole system he studies and its relative suitability (or not) to any range of student types or needs or to the prevailing realities of the street. That's not something he is thinking about. My advice on how to respond to such a claim: Nod your head with a polite smile and say, "Wow. That's great!" and just leave it at that.

> "While my enemy practiced the art of bragging, I practiced with my sword."
>
> -Akiyama Munenoshi

Practice.

Practice diligently.

Practice more than your enemies.

There is no substitute for diligent practice.

The next book in this series should be coming out soon:

Made in the USA
Middletown, DE
24 April 2018